To

From

SIMPLE
BLESSINGS

MOMENTS OF
QUIET REFLECTION

Publications International, Ltd.

Louis Weber, C.E.O.
Publications International, Ltd.
7373 North Cicero Avenue
Lincolnwood, Illinois 60646

Permission is never granted for commercial purposes.

Manufactured in China.

8 7 6 5 4 3 2 1

ISBN: 0-7853-2813-0

Many of the inspirations in this book were written and compiled by Pam Campbell, who serves as the Director of Publications for the American Association of Christian Counselors. She has also contributed to numerous magazines and books, including *Wisdom of Jesus* and *Rhythms of the Heart.*

Additional inspirations: Cecil C. Cole, Barbara Briggs Morrow, Anna Trimiew, Gary Wilde.

Acknowledgments:
The publisher gratefully acknowledges the kind permission granted to reprint the following copyrighted material. Should any copyright holder have been inadvertently omitted, they should apply to the publisher, who will be pleased to credit them in full in any subsequent editions.

Cover: From *All Desires Known,* © 1988, 1992, Janet Morley. Reprinted by permission of Morehouse Publishing.
Page 29: From *The Mother's Almanac* by Marguerite Kelly and Elia Parsons. © 1975 by Marguerite Kelly and Elia Parsons. Used by permission of Doubleday, a division of Bantam Doubleday Dell Publishing Group, Inc.

CONTENTS

The Blessings of Everyday Life

The Blessings of Community and Kinship

The Blessings of an Inner Life

The Blessings of Nature

THE BLESSINGS OF EVERYDAY LIFE

When learning to swim, many of us have stood on the edge of the pool with mom coaxing us to jump into her arms. Similarly, when we face the depths of everyday life, imagine God standing before us, arms outstretched, quietly saying, "Trust me, I'll catch you."

EVERYDAY LIFE

The true harvest of my daily life is somewhat intangible and indescribable as the tints of morning or evening. It is a little star dust caught, a segment of the rainbow which I have clutched.

HENRY DAVID THOREAU

EVERYDAY LIFE

There is a direct pleasure in seeing
work grow under one's hands day by
day, until at last it is finished.
This is the pleasure attaching to a
work of art or a manuscript or even
mere manual labor; and, of course,
the higher the work, the greater
pleasure it will give us.

ARTHUR SCHOPENHAUER

EVERYDAY LIFE

11

If you have built castles in the air, your work need not be lost; that is where they should be. Now put the foundations under them.

HENRY DAVID THOREAU

No matter how tightly the body may be chained to the wheel of daily duties, the spirit is free... to bear itself away from noise and vexation into the secret places of the mountains.

FRANK BOLLES

EVERYDAY LIFE

SIMPLE BLESSINGS

EVERYDAY LIFE

I long to accomplish a great and
noble task, but it is my chief duty
to accomplish humble tasks as
though they were great and noble.
The world is moved along, not only
by the mighty shoves of its heroes,
but also by the aggregate of the tiny
pushes of each honest worker.

ATTRIBUTED TO HELEN KELLER

EVERYDAY LIFE

I think laughter may be a form of courage. . . . As humans, we sometimes stand tall and look into the sun and laugh. And I think we are never more brave than when we do that.

LINDA ELLERBEE

It isn't the great big pleasures that count the most; it's making a great deal out of the little ones.

JEAN WEBSTER

EVERYDAY LIFE

WHAT GOD HATH PROMISED

God hath not promised
Skies always blue,
Flower-strewn pathways
All our lives through;
God hath not promised
Sun without rain,
Joy without sorrow,
Peace without pain.

But God hath promised
Strength for the day,
Rest for the labor,
Light for the way,
Grace for the trials,
Help from above,
Unfailing sympathy,
Undying love.

ANNIE JOHNSON FLINT

EVERYDAY LIFE

EVERYDAY LIFE

Hospitality doesn't imply a
four-course meal and an immaculate
home. It can be as simple as a loaf of
homemade bread, a bowl of soup,
and intimate conversation.

EVERYDAY LIFE

The world acquired a new interest
when birds appeared,
for the presence of birds at
any time is magical in effect.
They are magicians that transform
every scene; make of every
desert a garden of delights.

CHARLES C. ABBOTT

EVERYDAY LIFE

Books are the quietest and most
constant of friends;
they are the most accessible and
wisest of counsellors,
and the most patient of teachers.

CHARLES W. ELIOT

Music is the art of the prophets,
the only art that can calm the
agitations of the soul: it is one of the
most magnificent and delightful
presents God has given us.

MARTIN LUTHER

RULE OF CONDUCT

Do all the good you can,
By all the means you can,
In all the ways you can,
In all the places you can,
At all the times you can,
To all the people you can,
As long as ever you can.

JOHN WESLEY

Our smiles reflect the joy within us.
Perhaps if we practice smiling more
often, others will behold God in us
and find joy in our happiness.

EVERYDAY LIFE

One ought, every day at least,
to hear a little song, read a good
poem, see a fine picture, and,
if it were possible, to speak
a few reasonable words.

JOHANN W. VON GOETHE

If you have something to do,
someone to love, and something
to hope for, every day
becomes a celebration.

ANNA TRIMIEW

EVERYDAY LIFE

23

THE BLESSINGS OF COMMUNITY AND KINSHIP

Where we love is home,
Home that our feet may leave,
but not our hearts.
The chain may lengthen,
but it never parts.

OLIVER WENDELL HOLMES

SIMPLE BLESSINGS

COMMUNITY AND KINSHIP

In childhood, you and your sisters
start a relationship that becomes like
Grandmother's fine china.
When you take it out after years of
storage and dust it gently,
you'll discover that it's even more
beautiful than you remember.
And its value has increased
immeasurably over the years.

BARBARA BRIGGS MORROW

COMMUNITY AND KINSHIP

Uncles, and aunts, and cousins, are
all very well, and fathers and
mothers are not to be despised;
but a grandmother, at holiday time,
is worth them all.

FANNY FERN (SARA PAYSON PARTON)

COMMUNITY AND KINSHIP

There's a special kind of freedom
sisters enjoy. Freedom to share
innermost thoughts, to ask a favor,
to show their true feelings. The
freedom to simply be themselves.

ANONYMOUS

My sister and I were competitors
during our childhood. After all, we
had to share a lot—a bedroom,
clothes, mom and dad's attention.
Years later, we're vying for
something we never shared before—
intimacy and affection—the
blessings of sisterhood.

COMMUNITY AND KINSHIP

MY MOTHER

Who ran to help me when I fell
And would some pretty story tell,
Or kiss the place to make it well?
My Mother.

ANN TAYLOR

Nothing else ever will make you as
happy or as sad, as proud or as tired,
for nothing is quite as hard as
helping a person develop his own
individuality—especially while you
struggle to keep your own.

MARGUERITE KELLY AND ELIA PARSONS

COMMUNITY AND KINSHIP

My source for a comforting back scratch, my medic in removing a painful splinter, my driving teacher, my chemistry tutor, my porter when moving into the dorm, my escort down the aisle, and my first authority figure—these are just a few of my father's many roles.

COMMUNITY AND KINSHIP

All the feeling which my father could not put into words was in his hand—any dog, child or horse would recognize the kindness of it.

FREYA STARK

COMMUNITY AND KINSHIP

Oh, the comfort—the inexpressible
comfort of feeling safe with a
person—having neither to weigh
thoughts nor measure words,
but pouring them all right out,
just as they are, chaff and grain
together; certain that a faithful hand
will take them and sift them,
keep what is worth keeping,
and then with the breath
of kindness blow the rest away.

DINAH MARIA MULOCK CRAIK

COMMUNITY AND KINSHIP

SIMPLE BLESSINGS

COMMUNITY AND KINSHIP

Some people say a healthy marriage is
dependent on the ability of spouses to
meet each other's needs.
But when I think of the emotional
distress and anxiety I sometimes
experience, what an impossible challenge
for my spouse to live up to!
Our marriage is built on interdependence
but, thank goodness, it is also deeply
grounded in a commitment to the One
who can meet both our needs.

COMMUNITY AND KINSHIP

What greater thing is there for two
human souls, than to feel that they
are joined for life—to strengthen
each other in all labor,
to rest on each other in all sorrow,
to minister to each other in all pain,
to be one with each other in silent
unspeakable memories at
the moment of the last parting?

GEORGE ELIOT (MARY ANN EVANS CROSS)

COMMUNITY AND KINSHIP

Remembering the words of the Lord Jesus, for he himself said, "It is more blessed to give than to receive."

ACTS 20:35

I have decided to be attentive to others' needs rather than try to silence them. This means that I have to take time out of my busy schedule to listen. While I may experience some inconvenience, I expect the rewards of lending an ear to be deafening.

COMMUNITY AND KINSHIP

In friendship we find nothing false
or insincere; everything is
straightforward, and springs from
the heart.

MARCUS TULLIUS CICERO

COMMUNITY AND KINSHIP

The depth of a friendship can be
determined by the length of time
two friends can sit together
comfortably in silence.

COMMUNITY AND KINSHIP

But friendship is precious, not only
in the shade, but in the sunshine of
life; and thanks to a benevolent
arrangement of things, the greater
part of life is sunshine.

PRESIDENT THOMAS JEFFERSON,
FROM A LETTER TO MARIA COSWAY,
OCTOBER 12, 1786

Wherever you are, it is your own
friends who make your world.

WILLIAM JAMES

COMMUNITY AND KINSHIP

For memory has painted this perfect day
With colors that never fade,
And we find at the end of a perfect day
The soul of a friend we've made.

CARRIE JACOBS BOND

Sweet is the memory of distant
friends! Like the mellow rays of the
departing sun, it falls tenderly,
yet sadly, on the heart.

WASHINGTON IRVING

COMMUNITY AND KINSHIP

SIMPLE BLESSINGS

COMMUNITY AND KINSHIP

What a friend we have in Jesus
All our sins and griefs to bear....
Can we find a friend so faithful
Who will all our sorrows share?
Jesus knows our every weakness;
Take it to the Lord in prayer.

JOSEPH SCRIVEN,
"WHAT A FRIEND WE HAVE IN JESUS"

Whether we admit it or not, we all
long to feel welcomed and accepted
by others. Just as Jesus connected
with people outside his circle of
disciples, we need to connect with
people outside our comfort zone and
mirror God's acceptance of all people.

COMMUNITY AND KINSHIP

Well, the winter's gone, and I've
written no books, earned no
fortune; but I've made a friend
worth having and I'll try to keep
him all my life.

JO MARCH IN *LITTLE WOMEN*,
BY LOUISA MAY ALCOTT

I awoke this morning with devout
thanksgiving for my friends,
the old and the new.

RALPH WALDO EMERSON

COMMUNITY AND KINSHIP

THE BLESSINGS OF AN INNER LIFE

Lord, if we could see the future,
it would be easy to have hope.
Real hope is when we can't see the
end of the road, but still trust
you to lead us there.

CECIL COLE

SIMPLE BLESSINGS

AN INNER LIFE

Religious faith is not a storm cellar
to which men and women can flee
for refuge from the storms of life.
It is, instead, an inner spiritual
strength which enables them to face
those storms with hope and serenity.

SAM J. ERVIN, JR.

AN INNER LIFE

Nothing... is sweeter than love;
nothing higher, nothing stronger,
nothing larger, nothing more joyful,
nothing fuller, nothing better, in
heaven or on earth.

THOMAS À KEMPIS

Grace is not a strange, magic
substance which is subtly filtered
into our souls to act as a kind
of spiritual penicillin.
Grace is unity, oneness within
ourselves, oneness with God.

THOMAS MERTON

AN INNER LIFE

SHOWERS OF BLESSING

There shall be showers of blessing,
This is the promise of love;
There shall be seasons refreshing,
Sent from the Savior above.

Showers of blessing,
Showers of blessing we need;
Mercy drops around us are falling,
But for the showers we plead.

There shall be showers of blessing,
Precious reviving again;
Over the hills and the valleys
Sound of abundance of rain.

MAJOR DANIEL W. WHITTLE

AN INNER LIFE

I envy people who not only know
how to simplify their lives,
but actually lead lives of simplicity
without condemning those
of us who don't.

AN INNER LIFE

Storms sometimes arrive in our lives with hurricane-force winds. We feel as if our hearts are caught in the vortex. But just when we think we'll be destroyed, a still, small voice appears in the eye of the storm to remind us that we are not alone.

AN INNER LIFE

Do not worry about anything,
but in everything by prayer
and supplication with
thanksgiving let your requests be
made known to God.
And the peace of God, which
surpasses all understanding,
will guard your hearts and
your minds.

PHILIPPIANS 4:6–7

AN INNER LIFE

The guardian angels of life
sometimes fly so high as to be
beyond our sight, but they are
always looking down upon us.

JEAN PAUL RICHTER

Prayer can move mountains, they
say. But I've never seen a mountain
budge . . . except in an earthquake or
volcanic eruption. Maybe the results
of persistent prayer have the same
earthshaking, explosive results.

AN INNER LIFE

SIMPLE BLESSINGS

AN INNER LIFE

Slow me down, Lord!
Ease the pounding of my heart by
the quieting of my mind.
Steady my hurried pace with a vision
of the eternal reach of time.
Give me, amidst the confusion of my day,
the calmness of the everlasting hills.
Break the tensions of my nerves
and muscles with the soothing music of
singing streams that live in my memory.
Teach me the art of taking minute
vacations . . . of slowing down to look
at a flower, to chat with a friend,
to pat a dog, to read a few lines
from a good book.
Remind me each day of the fable of
the hare and the tortoise,

AN INNER LIFE

that I may know that the race is not
always to the swift; that there is more to
life than measuring its speed.
Let me look upward into the branches
of the towering oak and know that it
grew great and strong because it
grew slowly and well.
Slow me down, Lord, and inspire
me to send my roots deep into the
soil of life's enduring values that I may
grow toward the stars of
my greater destiny.

AUTHOR UNKNOWN

AN INNER LIFE

Blessed are the peacemakers, for
they will be called children of God.

MATTHEW 5:9

AN INNER LIFE

*L*et us not be content to wait and
see what will happen, but give us
the determination to make the
right things happen.

PETER MARSHALL, SENATE CHAPLAIN;
PRAYER OFFERED AT THE OPENING OF THE SESSION,
MARCH 10, 1948

*O*bserve how a child eagerly
offers her best efforts to her
parent or teacher.
The process of giving is never
complete until it becomes a mindset
and not just an action.

AN INNER LIFE

As storm clouds gathered,
Father, I used to run for cover,
panicked and picking
a favorite escape.
None of them worked for long,
Dear God, and none of
them kept me safe.
No more running then.
I see it clearly now:
Wherever I am standing is
a special place,
under the shadow of your
sheltering wing.

GARY WILDE

AN INNER LIFE

When I start to feel overwhelmed by
the problems and stresses of
everyday life, I know it's time to find
a quiet place where I can retreat and
rest my mind, body, and spirit.
Meditation is good for my soul.

AN INNER LIFE

THE BLESSINGS OF NATURE

If happiness consists in the number
of pleasing emotions that
occupy our mind—how true is it
that the contemplation of nature,
which always gives rise to these
emotions, is one of the great
sources of happiness.

THOMAS BELT

SIMPLE BLESSINGS

NATURE

How is it that the lonesome echo of
a loon across a deep, blue lake
at dusk restores such a sense of inner
calmness to my spirit?
Maybe it's because I slow down long
enough to see my reflection and
remember who created me.

NATURE

When we lack the society of our
fellow men, we take refuge in that of
animals, without always losing
by the change.

JEAN-HENRI FABRE

NATURE

*L*ord, I can hear your voice
in the bubbling brook,
see your beauty in the petals of a
flower, and feel your gentle breath in
the evening breeze and
in the soft kiss of a child.
Thank you for all of these gifts.

CECIL COLE

NATURE

Those who desire air and quick
recovery should go to the hills,
where the wind has a scent
of the sunbeams.

RICHARD JEFFERIES

NATURE

65

Autumn in the Smokies is
like going home. The smell of hickory
wood rising from a chimney warms
the crisp air and reminds me of
weekends in the mountains.
I have stealthily scouted behind rocks
and near rhododendrons for
black bears only to discover
them laughing at me from treetops.
I have waded in mountain streams till
my feet were numb, selecting smooth,
flat rocks for my garden.
I close my eyes, inhale, and breathe
in all these memories.

NATURE

SIMPLE BLESSINGS

NATURE

It's easy to praise you for your
majesty and power when we see
thundering waterfalls, crashing
ocean waves, or majestic sunsets.
Help us learn to praise you when we
see a dewdrop, a seedling, or an ant.

CECIL COLE

NATURE

I remember it—coming from a
swim and lying back in white
sand—the gift of a moment to rest,
to sit in reverie, to watch, to close
eyes and think of nothing but the
sound of breaking waves.
Yes, You were there with the sounds
and the sunshine, and
I am thankful.

GARY WILDE

NATURE

There are few of us who cannot
remember a front-yard garden which
seemed to us a very paradise
in childhood.

SARAH ORNE JEWETT

NATURE

No one can look at a pine-tree in
winter without knowing that spring
will come again in due time.

FRANK BOLLES

God passes through the thicket of
the world, and wherever his glance
falls he turns all things to beauty.

ST. JOHN OF THE CROSS

NATURE

The heart of the mountain is
the wild ravine where these two
streams mingle in perpetual
coolness and shadow.
No path leads to it and few are
the feet which have found a
way to its beauties.
There is a peculiar charm in a spot
unknown to the many.
Its loneliness endears it to the mind,
and gives its associations
a rarer flavor.

FRANK BOLLES

NATURE

NATURE

Surely there is something
in the unruffled calm
of nature that overawes our
little anxieties and doubts:
the sight of the deep-blue sky,
and the clustering stars above,
seem to impart a quiet to the mind.

JONATHAN EDWARDS

NATURE

When I first open my eyes upon the
morning meadows and look out
upon the beautiful world,
I thank God I am alive.

RALPH WALDO EMERSON

NATURE

Photo credits:

Front cover: "Mindy's Peonies" by Kim McDevitt/SuperStock.
C.W. Biedel, M.D./Photri: 8; Gay Bumgarner/Photo/Nats, Inc.:
59; Robert Clark/Transparencies, Inc.: 33; FPG International:
Laurance B. Aiuppy: 25, 45; Josef Beck: 13, 53; Buck Campbell:
19; Dennie Cody: 41; Gerald French: 10; Jeri Gleiter: 62; Steven
Gottlieb: 49; Haroldo de Faria Castro Cast: 17; Steve Hix: 69;
Frederick McKinney: 70; Barbara Peacock: 30; Miguel Sanchez
Salmeron: 34; Stephen Simpson: 65; Telegraph Colour Library: 9,
55, 73, 74; Arthur Tilley: 56; Toyohiro Yamada: Title page; Willie
Holdman/International Stock: 75; SuperStock: 18, 20, 31, 37, 38,
46, 50, 61, 63, 64, 67, 68, 76.

Additional photography: Siede/Preis Photography; Brian Warling.